THE DIABETIC CHEF'S TABLE: Gourmet Dishes for Blood Sugar Control

Mariah Blake

COPYRIGHT

All rights reserved. No part of this publication may be reproduced, distributed, or transmitted in any form or by any means, including photocopying, recording, or other electronic or mechanical methods, without the prior written permission of the publisher, except in the case of brief quotations embodied in critical reviews and certain other noncommercial uses permitted by copyright law.

Copyright © Mariah Blake, 2023.

TABLE OF CONTENTS

THE PURPOSE OF THIS BOOK 7
INTRODUCTION 10
CHAPTER ONE 14
Introduction to Diabetes and Blood Sugar Control 14
CHAPTER TWO 18
The Role of Nutrition in Managing Diabetes 18
CHAPTER THREE 23
Essential Cooking Techniques for Diabetics 23
CHAPTER FOUR 28
Gourmet Breakfasts for Healthy Mornings 28
CHAPTER FIVE 33
Satisfying Salads and Appetizers for Blood Sugar Balance 33
CHAPTER SIX 38

Hearty Soups and Stews: Comfort Food, Diabetic-Friendly Style..............................38

CHAPTER SEVEN......................................43

Flavorful Fish and Seafood: A Diabetic's Delight...43

CHAPTER EIGHT 48

Poultry Perfection: Delicious Chicken and Turkey Recipes for Diabetes......................48

CHAPTER NINE 52

Sensational Vegetarian and Vegan Options for Diabetic Diets...52

CHAPTER TEN 58

Mouthwatering Meat and Game: Diabetes-Compatible Recipes....................................58

CHAPTER ELEVEN 62

Wholesome Whole Grains: Creative Ways to Incorporate Them 62

CHAPTER TWELVE....................................67

Fantastic Side Dishes to Complement Your Main Course 67

CHAPTER THIRTEEN..............................72

Decadent Desserts without the Blood Sugar Spike 72

CHAPTER FOURTEEN 77

Savory Sauces, Dressings, and Marinades for Diabetic Cuisine 77

CHAPTER FIFTEEN 82

Guilt-Free Snacks and Small Bites for Diabetes Management 82

CHAPTER SIXTEEN 87

Celebratory Menus: Special Occasion Recipes for Diabetics 87

CHAPTER SEVENTEEN 92

Kid-Friendly Fare: Nurturing Diabetic Diets for Children 92

CHAPTER EIGHTEEN 98

Seasonal Delights: Recipes Inspired by Fresh Produce 98

CHAPTER NINETEEN 103

Quick and Easy Meals for Busy Diabetics 103

CHAPTER TWENTY 109

Dining Out the Diabetic Way: Tips and Tricks for Restaurant Success 109

CONCLUSION..114

THE PURPOSE OF THIS BOOK

The purpose of this book is to empower individuals with diabetes to embrace a gourmet culinary experience while effectively managing their blood sugar levels. This book aims to bridge the gap between gourmet cooking and diabetes management, demonstrating that delicious and satisfying meals can be prepared without compromising blood sugar control.

Through this book, readers will discover a collection of gourmet recipes specifically crafted to suit the needs of individuals with diabetes. The purpose is to provide a diverse range of tantalizing dishes that incorporate fresh, whole ingredients, and mindful cooking techniques. By offering detailed nutritional information and practical tips, the book guides readers in making informed choices, understanding the impact of ingredients and portion sizes on blood sugar levels.

"The Diabetic Chef's Table" seeks to inspire creativity in the kitchen by showcasing how gourmet cuisine can be adapted to meet the dietary requirements of individuals with diabetes. It encourages readers to explore new flavors, experiment with cooking techniques, and embrace a holistic approach to food that nourishes the body and delights the senses.

Additionally, the book aims to foster a sense of empowerment and confidence in individuals with diabetes. By providing the tools, knowledge, and inspiration to create gourmet meals that support blood sugar control, readers can take control of their dietary habits, improve their overall well-being, and experience the pleasure of gourmet dining in a diabetic-friendly way.

Ultimately, the purpose of "The Diabetic Chef's Table" is to transform the perception of diabetic cooking from a restrictive and mundane experience to one filled with culinary excitement and gourmet indulgence. It strives to show that managing diabetes does not mean sacrificing taste, flavor, or the joy of dining. With this book, individuals with diabetes can embark on a culinary adventure, embracing a delicious and balanced approach to food that enhances their health, satisfies their taste buds, and enriches their overall quality of life.

INTRODUCTION

This book is an invitation to embark on a culinary journey that combines the art of gourmet cooking with the science of blood sugar management. Here, we explore the exciting world of gourmet cuisine specifically tailored for individuals with diabetes, proving that exceptional flavor and optimal health can coexist on the same plate.

Living with diabetes does not mean compromising on the joys of dining. In fact, it presents an opportunity to embrace a culinary adventure that celebrates fresh, whole ingredients, mindful cooking techniques, and the power of delicious, nourishing meals. With "The Diabetic Chef's Table," we invite you to experience the pleasures of gourmet dining while effectively managing your blood sugar levels.

This book serves as your guide to a gourmet culinary experience designed to support blood sugar control. We understand that every bite matters, and that's why we have meticulously crafted a collection of recipes that prioritize flavor, nutrition, and balance. Each recipe has been thoughtfully developed and tested to ensure that it not only tantalizes your taste buds but also helps you maintain stable glucose levels.

Within these pages, you will discover a wealth of gourmet dishes spanning appetizers, main courses, side dishes, and even desserts. From vibrant salads and sumptuous seafood to comforting stews and indulgent treats, each recipe has been carefully crafted to suit the needs of individuals with diabetes. We have considered the impact of ingredients, portion sizes, and cooking methods to provide you with meals that nourish your body and delight your senses.

But this book is not just about recipes. It is a comprehensive resource that empowers you with knowledge, insights, and practical tips for successfully managing diabetes through gourmet cooking. We delve into the science behind blood sugar control, explore the role of nutrition, and offer guidance on portion sizes, carbohydrate counting, and mindful eating.

"The Diabetic Chef's Table" is not about restriction or deprivation. It is about embracing a holistic approach to food—one that celebrates the pleasure of dining while promoting optimal health. Through these gourmet recipes and the guidance provided, you will learn how to make informed choices, create balanced meals, and develop a deeper understanding of the impact of food on your blood sugar levels.

Whether you are a seasoned chef or an aspiring home cook, this book is for you. It is a testament to the fact that with the right knowledge, skills, and a dash of culinary creativity, you can transform your kitchen into a stage for gourmet delights that support your diabetes management goals.

So, get ready to embark on a journey of exquisite flavors, nourishing ingredients, and culinary mastery. Let "The Diabetic Chef's Table" be your companion as you embrace a world of gourmet cuisine tailored to your dietary needs, and let the joy of cooking and dining become an integral part of your diabetic lifestyle.

CHAPTER ONE

Introduction to Diabetes and Blood Sugar Control

In this chapter, we lay the foundation for understanding diabetes and the importance of blood sugar control. We provide an overview of the different types of diabetes, discuss the significance of maintaining healthy blood sugar levels, and introduce key concepts related to diabetes management.

Understanding Diabetes:

Diabetes is a chronic condition characterized by elevated blood sugar levels. There are three primary types of diabetes: type 1 diabetes, type 2 diabetes, and gestational diabetes. We delve into each type, exploring their causes, symptoms, and how they affect the body's ability to regulate blood sugar.

The Importance of Blood Sugar Control:

Managing blood sugar levels is essential for individuals with diabetes to maintain optimal health. In this section, we explain the potential consequences of uncontrolled blood sugar, such as organ damage, nerve problems, cardiovascular complications, and the increased risk of other health conditions. We highlight the benefits of effective blood sugar control, including improved energy levels, reduced risk of complications, and enhanced overall well-being.

Monitoring Blood Sugar:

Regular monitoring of blood sugar levels is a fundamental aspect of diabetes management. We discuss various methods of monitoring, including self-monitoring of blood glucose (SMBG) using glucometers, continuous glucose monitoring (CGM) systems, and the importance of keeping a log of readings. Additionally, we provide guidance on interpreting blood sugar levels and recognizing patterns to make informed decisions about diet, medication, and lifestyle adjustments.

Healthy Lifestyle Choices:

Maintaining a healthy lifestyle is crucial for individuals with diabetes. We discuss the significance of adopting a balanced diet, engaging in regular physical activity, managing stress levels, and getting adequate sleep. We emphasize the role of these lifestyle factors in achieving blood sugar control and overall well-being.

Diabetes Treatment Options:

We provide an overview of common treatment approaches for diabetes, including medication, insulin therapy, and lifestyle modifications. We explore the differences between oral medications and insulin injections, as well as the importance of individualized treatment plans tailored to each person's specific needs.

Nutrition for Blood Sugar Control:

Diet plays a vital role in managing diabetes and blood sugar levels. We introduce key principles of a diabetic-friendly diet, such as portion control, carbohydrate counting, glycemic index/load, and the importance of consuming a variety of nutrient-dense foods. We also touch upon the benefits of incorporating fiber-rich foods, lean proteins, healthy fats, and controlling sodium intake.

In this introductory chapter, we provide a comprehensive overview of diabetes and the significance of blood sugar control. By understanding the basics of diabetes, the importance of monitoring blood sugar, adopting a healthy lifestyle, and making informed dietary choices, readers will be equipped with the knowledge and motivation to embark on their journey towards optimal diabetes management and overall wellness.

CHAPTER TWO

The Role of Nutrition in Managing Diabetes

In this chapter, we explore the vital role that nutrition plays in managing diabetes. We delve into the impact of food choices on blood sugar levels, insulin sensitivity, weight management, and overall health. By understanding the principles of diabetic nutrition, readers can make informed decisions about their diet and optimize their diabetes management.

Understanding Carbohydrates:

Carbohydrates have the most significant effect on blood sugar levels, making them a crucial consideration for individuals with diabetes. We discuss the different types of carbohydrates, including simple sugars, complex carbohydrates, and fiber. Readers will learn about the concept of glycemic index (GI) and glycemic load (GL) and how they can help in selecting carbohydrates that have a minimal impact on blood sugar.

Balancing Carbohydrate Intake:

We provide practical strategies for carbohydrate intake management, including carbohydrate counting, meal planning, and portion control. Readers will learn how to distribute carbohydrates throughout the day to prevent blood sugar spikes and achieve better glycemic control. We also highlight the importance of considering the quality of carbohydrates, such as choosing whole grains over refined grains.

The Power of Protein:

Protein is an essential macronutrient that plays a significant role in managing diabetes. We discuss the benefits of protein in promoting satiety, stabilizing blood sugar levels, and supporting muscle health. Readers will learn about the best sources of protein, such as lean meats, poultry, fish, legumes, and dairy products, and how to incorporate them into their meals.

Healthy Fats for Diabetes:

Contrary to popular belief, not all fats are harmful for individuals with diabetes. We explore the role of healthy fats, such as monounsaturated fats and polyunsaturated fats, in improving insulin sensitivity, reducing inflammation, and supporting heart health. We provide guidance on incorporating sources of healthy fats, such as avocados, nuts, seeds, and olive oil, into a diabetes-friendly diet.

The Importance of Fiber:

Fiber offers numerous benefits for individuals with diabetes. We discuss the different types of fiber, soluble and insoluble, and their impact on blood sugar control, digestion, and heart health. Readers will learn about high-fiber food sources, including fruits, vegetables, whole grains, and legumes, and how to increase their fiber intake to achieve better diabetes management.

Vitamins, Minerals, and Antioxidants:

We highlight the importance of obtaining essential vitamins, minerals, and antioxidants through a well-rounded diet. These nutrients play a vital role in overall health, immune function, and managing diabetes-related complications. Readers will learn about key sources of these nutrients and how to incorporate them into their meals.

By understanding the impact of carbohydrates, protein, fats, fiber, and essential nutrients, readers can make informed dietary choices to control blood sugar levels, enhance insulin sensitivity, achieve a healthy weight, and improve overall well-being. Through a balanced and mindful approach to nutrition, individuals with diabetes can effectively manage their condition and optimize their health outcomes.

CHAPTER THREE

Essential Cooking Techniques for Diabetics

Here, we focus on essential cooking techniques that are beneficial for individuals with diabetes. By understanding and implementing these techniques, readers can prepare delicious, diabetes-friendly meals while maximizing flavor, nutritional value, and blood sugar control.

1. Grilling and Roasting:

Grilling and roasting are excellent cooking methods for individuals with diabetes as they require minimal added fats and can enhance the natural flavors of food. We discuss the benefits of grilling and roasting various proteins, such as lean meats, poultry, and fish, as well as vegetables. Readers will learn about proper seasoning, marinating techniques, and optimal cooking times to achieve mouthwatering results.

2. Steaming:

Steaming is a gentle and healthful cooking technique that preserves the natural nutrients and flavors of foods. We explore the versatility of steaming, from vegetables and seafood to whole grains and even desserts. Readers will discover tips for steaming different ingredients, such as using steamer baskets, parchment paper, or foil, and how to incorporate herbs, spices, and citrus to add extra flavor.

3. Stir-Frying:

Stir-frying is a quick and flavorful cooking technique that can be adapted to suit a diabetes-friendly diet. We discuss the benefits of stir-frying vegetables, lean proteins, and whole grains using minimal oil and high heat. Readers will learn about the importance of prepping ingredients ahead of time, using a variety of colorful vegetables, and incorporating low-sodium sauces and seasonings to create delicious stir-fry dishes.

4. Baking and Broiling:

Baking and broiling are versatile cooking techniques that can be used to prepare a wide range of diabetic-friendly meals. We explore baking techniques for lean meats, poultry, fish, and vegetables, focusing on using herbs, spices, and marinades to add flavor. Additionally, we discuss the benefits of broiling for quick and convenient cooking, especially for open-faced sandwiches, fish fillets, and vegetable gratins.

5. Poaching:

Poaching is a gentle cooking technique that allows for the preparation of tender and flavorful dishes without adding excessive fats. We discuss the benefits of poaching proteins such as fish, chicken, and eggs. Readers will learn about using flavorful liquids like broth, citrus juices, or aromatic herbs to enhance the taste of poached dishes while maintaining their nutritional integrity.

6. Sautéing:

Sautéing is a cooking technique that involves quickly cooking food in a small amount of fat over high heat. We explore sautéing techniques for vegetables, proteins, and whole grains, focusing on using heart-healthy fats like olive oil or coconut oil. Readers will learn about proper heat control, using a non-stick pan, and incorporating herbs, spices, and low-sodium sauces to enhance the flavors of sautéed dishes.

7. Slow Cooking:

Slow cooking is an excellent technique for individuals with diabetes as it allows for hands-off preparation and yields tender, flavorful meals. We discuss the benefits of using a slow cooker or crockpot to prepare soups, stews, and braised dishes. Readers will learn about selecting lean cuts of meat, incorporating an array of vegetables, and using herbs and spices to create rich and satisfying slow-cooked meals.

By mastering these techniques, readers can prepare a variety of delicious and diabetes-friendly meals while maximizing flavor, nutrition, and blood sugar control. Whether grilling, roasting, steaming, stir-frying, baking, poaching, sautéing, or slow cooking, individuals with diabetes can embrace these techniques to create wholesome, flavorful dishes that contribute to their overall well-being.

CHAPTER FOUR

Gourmet Breakfasts for Healthy Mornings

In this chapter, we focus on gourmet breakfast options that are not only delicious but also promote a healthy start to the day for individuals with diabetes. By incorporating quality ingredients, balanced macronutrients, and creative flavor combinations, readers can enjoy satisfying breakfasts that support stable blood sugar levels and provide sustained energy throughout the morning.

1. Overnight Oats with a Twist:

Overnight oats are a versatile and convenient breakfast option. We explore various combinations of whole grains, such as rolled oats or quinoa, mixed with unsweetened almond milk or Greek yogurt. Readers will discover the art of adding flavor through spices, fruits, and healthy toppings like nuts, seeds, or a drizzle of sugar-free syrup. These customizable overnight oats are perfect for those who prefer to prepare breakfast the night before.

2. Protein-Packed Egg Dishes:

Eggs are a fantastic source of protein and can be the centerpiece of a gourmet diabetic breakfast. We explore different cooking methods such as scrambled, poached, or baked eggs. Readers will learn how to pair eggs with vegetables, herbs, and low-fat cheeses for a nutrient-rich and satisfying meal. We also provide tips for creating flavorful omelets or frittatas with a variety of fillings.

3. Wholesome Smoothie Bowls:

Smoothie bowls offer a refreshing and nutritious breakfast option. We discuss the importance of balancing carbohydrates, proteins, and healthy fats in smoothie bowl recipes. Readers will learn about using a base of low-glycemic fruits, like berries or avocado, and incorporating protein sources such as Greek yogurt or plant-based protein powders. Toppings such as nuts, seeds, granola, or fresh fruits add texture and additional nutrients.

4. Creative Whole Grain Pancakes and Waffles:

Indulge in gourmet pancakes and waffles without compromising blood sugar control. We explore recipes using whole grain flours, such as buckwheat, oat, or almond flour. Readers will discover the art of adding natural sweetness with ingredients like mashed bananas, unsweetened applesauce, or spices like cinnamon and nutmeg. Toppings such as sugar-free syrups, fresh berries, or a dollop of Greek yogurt can elevate these breakfast treats.

5. Savory Breakfast Wraps and Sandwiches:

Move beyond traditional sweet breakfast options with savory wraps and sandwiches. We discuss using whole grain tortillas or bread as a base and filling them with lean proteins such as smoked salmon, turkey, or grilled vegetables. Readers will explore options for adding flavor through spreads like hummus, avocado, or sugar-free pesto. These savory breakfast options provide a satisfying and balanced start to the day.

6. Nutrient-Dense Breakfast Parfaits:

Breakfast parfaits offer a beautiful and nutritious way to start the morning. We explore layering low-sugar Greek yogurt or cottage cheese with fresh fruits, nuts, and seeds. Readers will learn how to create different flavor profiles using combinations such as tropical fruits with coconut flakes or mixed berries with crushed almonds. These parfaits provide a balance of carbohydrates, proteins, and healthy fats.

In this chapter, we have explored gourmet breakfast options for individuals with diabetes that go beyond the ordinary. By incorporating a variety of wholesome ingredients, balancing macronutrients, and experimenting with creative flavor combinations, readers can elevate their breakfast experience while supporting stable blood sugar levels and overall health. These gourmet breakfasts offer a delightful start to the day, setting the tone for healthy choices and sustained energy throughout the morning.

CHAPTER FIVE

Satisfying Salads and Appetizers for Blood Sugar Balance

Maintaining balanced blood sugar levels is crucial for overall health, especially for individuals with diabetes or those who are looking to prevent blood sugar imbalances. One effective way to support blood sugar balance is through a diet that includes nutritious salads and appetizers. These dishes can be both satisfying and delicious while providing essential nutrients and helping to stabilize blood sugar levels. Here, we explore some ideas for satisfying salads and appetizers that are perfect for promoting blood sugar balance.

3. Colorful Garden Salad:

A colorful garden salad is not only visually appealing but also packed with nutrients. Start with a base of fresh leafy greens such as spinach or mixed greens. Add an assortment of colorful vegetables like bell peppers, cherry tomatoes, cucumber slices, grated carrots, and thinly sliced red onions. To add some protein and healthy fats, top the salad with grilled chicken, boiled eggs, avocado slices, or a sprinkling of nuts and seeds. For dressing, choose a homemade vinaigrette using olive oil, lemon juice, and a touch of Dijon mustard. This vibrant salad provides a variety of fiber, vitamins, minerals, and antioxidants to help maintain stable blood sugar levels.

2. Quinoa and Vegetable Stuffed Peppers:

Stuffed peppers make for an excellent appetizer or a light meal option. Prepare a filling by combining cooked quinoa with sautéed vegetables such as zucchini, mushrooms, onions, and spinach. Season the mixture with herbs and spices like garlic, cumin, and paprika for added flavor. Slice bell peppers in half, remove the seeds and membranes, and stuff them with the quinoa and vegetable mixture. Place the stuffed peppers in the oven and bake until the peppers are tender and lightly browned. This dish offers a balanced combination of protein, fiber, and complex carbohydrates, which contribute to stable blood sugar levels.

3. Chickpea and Avocado Salad:

Chickpeas are a fantastic ingredient for blood sugar balance as they have a low glycemic index and are rich in fiber and plant-based protein. Create a refreshing salad by combining cooked chickpeas with diced avocado, cherry tomatoes, chopped cucumbers, and fresh herbs like cilantro or parsley. Drizzle the salad with a tangy dressing made from lemon juice, olive oil, and a pinch of sea salt. The fiber content in chickpeas and the healthy fats from avocado help slow down digestion and prevent rapid spikes in blood sugar levels.

4. Cucumber Roll-Ups:

Cucumber roll-ups are a creative and healthy appetizer option that is easy to prepare. Start by slicing a cucumber lengthwise into thin strips using a mandoline or a vegetable peeler. Spread a layer of hummus or mashed avocado on each cucumber strip and then add a filling such as smoked salmon, grilled chicken, or a mixture of diced vegetables. Roll up the cucumber strips, securing them with toothpicks if needed. These refreshing roll-ups provide hydration, fiber, and a balanced combination of nutrients that support blood sugar balance.

5. Roasted Beet and Goat Cheese Salad:

Beets are known for their blood sugar-regulating properties as they are low in carbohydrates and high in fiber. To prepare a satisfying salad, roast beets in the oven until tender, and then allow them to cool. Slice the roasted beets and combine them with mixed greens, crumbled goat cheese, and a handful of walnuts or pecans for added crunch. Drizzle the salad with a light dressing made from balsamic vinegar, extra virgin olive oil, and a touch of honey or a sugar substitute if desired. This salad provides a balance of flavors and textures while promoting blood sugar stability.

When selecting ingredients for salads and appetizers to support blood sugar balance, it is essential to focus on whole foods, lean proteins, healthy fats, and high-fiber options. These choices contribute to slower digestion, increased satiety, and minimized blood sugar spikes. By incorporating satisfying salads and appetizers into your diet, you can take a step towards maintaining optimal blood sugar levels while enjoying delicious and nutritious meals.

CHAPTER SIX

Hearty Soups and Stews: Comfort Food, Diabetic-Friendly Style

When it comes to comfort food, few things can match the warmth and satisfaction of a hearty bowl of soup or stew. If you're following a diabetic-friendly diet or aiming to maintain stable blood sugar levels, there are plenty of options available that offer both comfort and nutritional balance. By incorporating low-glycemic index ingredients, lean proteins, and an array of flavorful vegetables, you can create delicious soups and stews that are suitable for blood sugar control. Let's explore some ideas for hearty soups and stews that provide comfort and nourishment without compromising your dietary goals.

1. Vegetable and Lentil Soup:

Packed with fiber and plant-based protein, a vegetable and lentil soup is an excellent choice for a diabetic-friendly meal. Combine a variety of colorful vegetables like carrots, celery, zucchini, and bell peppers with red or green lentils. Season it with herbs and spices like cumin, paprika, and bay leaves for added depth of flavor. Serve it with a side of whole-grain bread for a complete and satisfying meal.

2. Chicken and Vegetable Stew:

Loaded with lean protein, chicken, and a medley of vegetables, this stew is both comforting and diabetes-friendly. Start by browning chicken breast or thighs in a pot, then add in onions, garlic, carrots, celery, and diced tomatoes. Season with herbs like thyme, rosemary, and bay leaves. Allow it to simmer until the flavors meld together, and the chicken is tender. Serve it with a side of steamed greens or cauliflower rice for a well-rounded meal.

3. Beef and Barley Soup:

Barley, a whole grain, adds a nutty flavor and chewy texture to this classic soup. Begin by browning lean beef cubes in a pot with onions and garlic. Add in low-sodium beef broth, diced tomatoes, and a generous amount of vegetables such as carrots, celery, and mushrooms. Simmer until the beef is tender and the flavors meld together. Finally, add cooked barley to the soup and let it simmer for a few more minutes. Enjoy this comforting and filling soup as a main course.

4. Fish Chowder:

Fish chowder can be a light and flavorful option for those seeking a diabetic-friendly soup. Use a combination of fish like cod, haddock, or salmon and combine them with low-sodium vegetable or fish broth. Add in a variety of colorful vegetables such as potatoes, corn, onions, and celery. Season with dill, thyme, and a splash of lemon juice for brightness. Finish with a touch of low-fat milk or cream substitute to create a creamy texture without excessive fat and calories.

5. Minestrone Soup:

A classic Italian soup, minestrone, can be easily adapted to be diabetic-friendly. Start with a vegetable broth base and add a variety of vegetables like carrots, celery, zucchini, green beans, and spinach. Incorporate kidney beans or other legumes for added fiber and plant-based protein. Season with Italian herbs like oregano, basil, and thyme. Serve it with a sprinkle of grated Parmesan cheese and a slice of whole-grain bread on the side.

When preparing soups and stews, be mindful of the overall carbohydrate content and adjust the portions of starchy ingredients accordingly. It's also essential to use low-sodium broths and seasonings to keep sodium levels in check. By selecting wholesome ingredients and using flavorful herbs and spices, you can create comforting soups and stews that are both delicious and diabetic-friendly.

CHAPTER SEVEN

Flavorful Fish and Seafood: A Diabetic's Delight

Fish and seafood are not only delicious and versatile but can also be a diabetic's delight due to their numerous health benefits and low impact on blood sugar levels. Packed with lean protein, healthy fats, and essential nutrients, fish and seafood provide a flavorful and nutritious option for individuals managing diabetes. Let's explore the reasons why fish and seafood are a great choice and some ideas for preparing them in a diabetic-friendly manner.

1. Lean Protein Powerhouses:

Fish and seafood are excellent sources of lean protein, which is essential for maintaining stable blood sugar levels and promoting satiety. Unlike high-fat meats, fish and seafood provide protein without the added saturated fat. Protein helps slow down digestion and the release of glucose into the bloodstream, preventing blood sugar spikes. Incorporating fish and seafood into your meals can support balanced blood sugar levels throughout the day.

2. Omega-3 Fatty Acids for Heart Health:

Fatty fish such as salmon, trout, sardines, and mackerel are rich in omega-3 fatty acids. These healthy fats have been shown to improve heart health, reduce inflammation, and lower the risk of cardiovascular diseases, which are commonly associated with diabetes. Including fish high in omega-3 fatty acids in your diet can contribute to overall well-being and help manage diabetes-related complications.

3. Low in Carbohydrates:

Fish and seafood are naturally low in carbohydrates, making them an ideal choice for individuals concerned about blood sugar control. Unlike high-carbohydrate foods that can cause blood sugar spikes, fish and seafood have minimal impact on glucose levels. This makes them a great addition to a diabetic meal plan, as they provide essential nutrients without raising blood sugar excessively.

4. Versatile and Flavorful:

Fish and seafood offer a wide variety of flavors and textures, allowing for endless culinary possibilities. Whether you prefer delicate white fish, rich salmon, or succulent shellfish, there are numerous options to explore. You can bake, grill, steam, or sauté fish and seafood with a variety of herbs, spices, and marinades to create a diverse range of delicious meals. Experimenting with different flavors and cooking methods can keep your diabetic-friendly meals exciting and satisfying.

5. Diabetic-Friendly Recipe Ideas:

a. **Baked Lemon Herb Salmon:**
Marinate salmon fillets with lemon juice, minced garlic, and a blend of fresh herbs like dill, parsley, and thyme. Bake the salmon in the oven until flaky and serve with a side of steamed vegetables or a mixed green salad.

b. **Grilled Shrimp Skewers:**
Thread marinated shrimp onto skewers, alternating with chunks of colorful bell peppers, onions, and cherry tomatoes. Grill until the shrimp are cooked through and serve with a squeeze of fresh lime juice.

c. **Tuna Salad Lettuce Wraps:**
Mix canned tuna with diced celery, red onion, and a dollop of Greek yogurt or mashed avocado for creaminess. Season with lemon juice, salt, and pepper. Scoop the tuna salad onto

lettuce leaves and roll them up for a refreshing and low-carb meal.

d. **Garlic and Herb Cod:**
Sauté cod fillets in a pan with minced garlic, fresh herbs like rosemary and thyme, and a drizzle of olive oil. Serve the cod with a side of roasted vegetables or a quinoa and vegetable pilaf.

Always remember to choose fresh, high-quality fish and seafood and be mindful of portion sizes. Incorporating fish and seafood into your diabetic meal plan not only adds variety and flavor but also provides essential nutrients and health benefits. With their lean protein content, low carbohydrate impact, and omega-3 fatty acids, fish and seafood can be a delightful addition to a diabetic's diet.

CHAPTER EIGHT

Poultry Perfection: Delicious Chicken and Turkey Recipes for Diabetes

Poultry, such as chicken and turkey, is a versatile and delicious protein option that can be enjoyed by individuals managing diabetes. Packed with lean protein, essential nutrients, and low in saturated fat, poultry offers a wide range of possibilities for creating flavorful and diabetic-friendly meals. Whether grilled, baked, or roasted, chicken and turkey can be prepared in various ways to suit your taste preferences. Let's explore some poultry perfection with delicious chicken and turkey recipes that are ideal for diabetes management.

1. Grilled Lemon Herb Chicken:

Marinate boneless, skinless chicken breasts in a mixture of fresh lemon juice, minced garlic, olive oil, and a blend of herbs like rosemary, thyme, and oregano. Allow the chicken to marinate for at least 30 minutes, then grill it to perfection. The tangy and aromatic flavors of this dish will leave you satisfied without causing blood sugar spikes. Serve with a side of grilled vegetables or a fresh salad.

2. Baked Turkey Meatballs:

Combine lean ground turkey with minced onions, garlic, whole-grain breadcrumbs, and a selection of herbs and spices such as parsley, basil, and paprika. Shape the mixture into meatballs and bake them in the oven until golden brown. These turkey meatballs are a low-carb alternative to traditional beef meatballs and can be served with zucchini noodles or whole-grain pasta tossed in a light tomato sauce.

3. Herb-Roasted Chicken Thighs:

Season skin-on, bone-in chicken thighs with a mixture of dried herbs like thyme, oregano, and sage, along with minced garlic, olive oil, salt, and pepper. Roast the chicken thighs in the oven until the skin is crispy and the meat is tender. This dish offers robust flavors while maintaining portion control by using skin-on, bone-in cuts. Pair it with a side of steamed vegetables or a quinoa pilaf.

4. Turkey and Vegetable Stir-Fry:

Sauté sliced turkey breast or turkey tenderloins with an assortment of colorful vegetables such as bell peppers, broccoli, snap peas, and carrots. Flavor the stir-fry with a low-sodium soy sauce or a combination of ginger, garlic, and a splash of low-sodium chicken broth. Serve over a bed of cauliflower rice or brown rice for a satisfying and low-glycemic meal.

5. Lemon Rosemary Roast Chicken:

Rub a whole chicken with a mixture of lemon zest, minced garlic, fresh rosemary leaves, olive oil, salt, and pepper. Roast the chicken in the oven until it reaches an internal temperature of 165°F (74°C). The combination of lemon and rosemary infuses the chicken with delightful flavors. Serve with a side of roasted vegetables or a mixed green salad.

Always remove the skin from poultry to reduce saturated fat content and control portion sizes. Also, experiment with different herbs, spices, and marinades to add variety to your poultry dishes. By choosing lean cuts of chicken and turkey and incorporating them into your meals, you can enjoy a protein-rich diet that supports stable blood sugar levels and overall health.

Try to consult with your healthcare provider or a registered dietitian for personalized dietary advice and portion recommendations based on your specific needs and health goals.

CHAPTER NINE

Sensational Vegetarian and Vegan Options for Diabetic Diets

Following a vegetarian or vegan diet can be a healthy and fulfilling choice for individuals managing diabetes. By incorporating a variety of plant-based foods, you can create sensational meals that are rich in fiber, low in saturated fats, and have a low impact on blood sugar levels. Vegetarian and vegan options offer an abundance of nutrient-dense ingredients that support blood sugar control, provide essential nutrients, and promote overall well-being. Let's explore some sensational vegetarian and vegan options for diabetic diets.

1. Plant-Based Proteins:

Vegetarian and vegan diets rely on plant-based proteins to replace animal products. Incorporating protein-rich foods such as legumes (beans, lentils, and chickpeas), tofu, tempeh, seitan, and edamame provides essential amino acids while being low in saturated fats. These protein sources have a minimal effect on blood sugar levels and help promote satiety.

2. Abundant Fiber:

Fiber plays a crucial role in managing blood sugar levels as it slows down the digestion and absorption of carbohydrates. Vegetarian and vegan diets, with their emphasis on whole grains, fruits, vegetables, and legumes, are naturally high in fiber. Including a variety of fiber-rich foods, such as leafy greens, broccoli, quinoa, brown rice, and chia seeds, can support stable blood sugar levels and aid in maintaining a healthy weight.

3. Colorful Vegetable Medleys:

Vegetarian and vegan diets offer a wide array of colorful vegetables that can be combined in exciting ways. Roasted vegetables, stir-fries, vegetable curries, and salads can be packed with flavor and essential nutrients. Experiment with different vegetable combinations, herbs, and spices to create sensational dishes that are satisfying and blood sugar-friendly.

4. Whole Grains and Legumes:

Incorporating whole grains and legumes into meals is an excellent way to add complex carbohydrates, fiber, and plant-based proteins. Whole grains like quinoa, brown rice, barley, and whole-wheat bread have a lower impact on blood sugar compared to refined grains. Legumes, such as lentils, beans, and chickpeas, are rich in fiber and protein, providing sustained energy without causing blood sugar spikes.

5. Nutritious Nuts and Seeds:

Nuts and seeds are a great source of healthy fats, protein, and essential nutrients. They can be enjoyed as snacks or incorporated into meals for added texture and flavor. Almonds, walnuts, chia seeds, flaxseeds, and pumpkin seeds are examples of nutrient-dense options that provide healthy fats, fiber, and important vitamins and minerals.

6. Sensational Recipe Ideas:

a. **Lentil and Vegetable Curry:**
Combine red or green lentils with a variety of vegetables such as bell peppers, cauliflower, carrots, and spinach. Cook in a flavorful curry sauce made from coconut milk, turmeric, ginger, and cumin. Serve over brown rice or with whole-wheat naan bread.

b. **Roasted Vegetable Quinoa Salad:**
Roast an assortment of colorful vegetables like bell peppers, zucchini, eggplant, and cherry tomatoes. Toss them with cooked quinoa, fresh herbs, lemon juice, and a drizzle of olive oil. Add some toasted almonds or crumbled feta cheese for extra flavor.

c. **Tofu Stir-Fry:**
Sauté tofu cubes with a mix of your favorite vegetables such as broccoli, snap peas, mushrooms, and carrots. Add low-sodium soy sauce, garlic, and ginger for a savory Asian-inspired flavor. Serve over brown rice or whole-wheat noodles.

d. **Chickpea Salad Wraps:**
Mash chickpeas with mashed avocado, diced cucumbers, cherry tomatoes, red onion, and a squeeze of lemon juice. Season with salt, pepper, and fresh herbs like cilantro. Wrap the mixture in large lettuce leaves for a refreshing and low-carb meal.

Don't forget to monitor your carbohydrate intake and portion sizes to maintain blood sugar control. These sensational vegetarian and vegan options provide a wealth of nutrients, fiber, and plant-based proteins, making them suitable choices for individuals managing diabetes. By incorporating a variety of plant-based ingredients, you can create delicious, satisfying meals that support stable blood sugar levels and contribute to overall health and well-being.

CHAPTER TEN

Mouthwatering Meat and Game: Diabetes-Compatible Recipes

For individuals managing diabetes, incorporating lean cuts of meat and game into their diet can provide a mouthwatering and satisfying option. While it's important to be mindful of portion sizes and cooking methods, meat and game can be part of a diabetes-compatible meal plan. These protein-rich options offer essential nutrients, help maintain satiety, and have minimal impact on blood sugar levels. Let's explore some mouthwatering recipes featuring meat and game that are suitable for individuals with diabetes.

1. Grilled Herb-Marinated Chicken Breast:

Marinate chicken breasts with a mixture of olive oil, minced garlic, fresh herbs like rosemary and thyme, lemon juice, salt, and pepper. Grill the chicken until it reaches an internal temperature of 165°F (74°C). Serve with a side of steamed vegetables or a mixed green salad for a balanced and diabetes-friendly meal.

2. Baked Salmon with Lemon and Dill:

Place salmon fillets on a baking sheet lined with parchment paper. Season with lemon zest, fresh dill, salt, and pepper. Bake in a preheated oven at 400°F (200°C) for about 12-15 minutes or until the salmon flakes easily with a fork. Serve with a side of roasted asparagus or quinoa for a nutritious and omega-3-rich dish.

3. Grilled Turkey Burgers with Portobello Mushrooms:

Prepare turkey burger patties using lean ground turkey mixed with chopped onions, garlic, parsley, and your choice of seasonings. Grill the burgers until cooked through. While the burgers are grilling, brush portobello mushroom caps with olive oil, salt, and pepper, and grill them until tender. Serve the turkey burgers on whole-grain buns or lettuce wraps, topped with the grilled portobello mushrooms and your favorite burger toppings.

4. Bison Stir-Fry with Vegetables:

Slice lean bison steak into thin strips and marinate with low-sodium soy sauce, minced garlic, ginger, and a touch of honey. In a hot skillet or wok, stir-fry the marinated bison with an assortment of colorful vegetables like bell peppers, broccoli, carrots, and snap peas. Serve over brown rice or cauliflower rice for a delicious and protein-packed meal.

5. Grilled Venison Tenderloin with Herb Butter:

Season venison tenderloin with a mixture of dried herbs such as thyme, rosemary, and garlic powder, along with salt and pepper. Grill the tenderloin to your desired level of doneness and let it rest before slicing. Top the slices with a pat of herb butter made with fresh herbs, garlic, and unsalted butter. Serve with a side of roasted root vegetables or a green salad for a flavorful and nutrient-dense dish.

Endeavour to choose lean cuts of meat, trim excess fat, and opt for healthier cooking methods such as grilling, baking, or broiling. Additionally, be mindful of portion sizes and balance your meal with a variety of non-starchy vegetables and whole grains to create a well-rounded and diabetes-compatible plate.

By selecting lean cuts of meat and game, incorporating flavorful herbs and spices, and pairing them with nutritious sides, you can create mouthwatering dishes that are suitable for individuals managing diabetes. Enjoy the richness and satisfaction of meat and game while maintaining stable blood sugar levels and supporting your overall health.

CHAPTER ELEVEN

Wholesome Whole Grains: Creative Ways to Incorporate Them

Wholesome whole grains are a valuable addition to any diet, and they can play a particularly important role in managing diabetes. Packed with fiber, essential nutrients, and a slower release of carbohydrates compared to refined grains, whole grains offer numerous health benefits and help maintain stable blood sugar levels. By incorporating a variety of whole grains into your meals, you can enjoy their nutritional goodness and explore creative and delicious ways to incorporate them. Let's discover some creative ideas for incorporating wholesome whole grains into your diet.

1. Overnight Oats:

Start your day off right with a satisfying bowl of overnight oats. Mix rolled oats with your choice of milk (dairy or plant-based), a touch of sweetener like honey or maple syrup, and add-ins such as chia seeds, flaxseeds, or chopped nuts. Let the mixture sit in the refrigerator overnight, and in the morning, top it with fresh fruits, a sprinkle of cinnamon, and a dollop of yogurt. Overnight oats provide a hearty and fiber-rich breakfast option.

2. Quinoa Salad:

Quinoa is a versatile and protein-packed whole grain that can be used in various salads. Cook quinoa according to package instructions and let it cool. Toss the quinoa with an assortment of colorful vegetables, such as diced cucumbers, cherry tomatoes, bell peppers, and fresh herbs. Add a tangy dressing made with lemon juice, olive oil, and your favorite herbs and seasonings. Quinoa salad can be enjoyed as a refreshing side dish or a light meal on its own.

3. Whole Grain Wraps:

Swap out traditional refined flour tortillas for whole grain wraps when making sandwiches or wraps. Look for whole wheat, whole grain, or multigrain options that are higher in fiber and lower in refined carbohydrates. Fill your wraps with lean protein, plenty of vegetables, and a flavorful spread like hummus or avocado. Enjoy a wholesome and satisfying meal that's packed with nutrients.

4. Brown Rice Stir-Fry:

When preparing a stir-fry, opt for brown rice instead of white rice. Brown rice is a whole grain that retains the bran and germ, making it higher in fiber and nutrients. Cook the brown rice according to package instructions and stir-fry it with a medley of colorful vegetables, lean protein, and a low-sodium sauce. Add some aromatic spices like ginger and garlic for an extra kick of flavor. Brown rice stir-fry offers a balanced and filling meal that's rich in fiber.

5. Whole Grain Baked Goods:

Experiment with baking by incorporating whole grain flours into your recipes. Replace some or all of the refined white flour with whole wheat flour, spelt flour, or oat flour in your favorite muffins, bread, or pancake recipes. You can also incorporate other whole grains like rolled oats or quinoa flour for added texture and nutritional benefits. These swaps increase the fiber content and make your baked goods more diabetes-friendly.

6. Ancient Grain Bowls:

Explore the world of ancient grains such as farro, bulgur, freekeh, and amaranth. Cook these grains according to package instructions and use them as a base for nourishing grain bowls. Top the cooked grains with a variety of roasted or sautéed vegetables, lean protein like grilled chicken or tofu, and a flavorful dressing or sauce. Ancient grain bowls provide a wholesome and satisfying meal that's packed with nutrients.

Practice portion control and balance your meals with a variety of vegetables, lean proteins, and healthy fats. Wholesome whole grains offer endless possibilities for creative and delicious meals. By incorporating them into your diet, you'll enjoy their nutritional benefits and contribute to your overall well-being, all while managing your blood sugar levels effectively.

CHAPTER TWELVE

Fantastic Side Dishes to Complement Your Main Course

A fantastic side dish can elevate a meal and add a burst of flavor, texture, and nutrition to complement your main course. Whether you're looking for something light and refreshing or hearty and comforting, there are endless options to choose from. These side dishes can be paired with various main courses, accommodating different dietary preferences and needs. Let's explore some fantastic side dishes that can take your meal to the next level.

1. Roasted Vegetables:

Roasting vegetables brings out their natural sweetness and creates a caramelized, flavorful dish. Toss an assortment of colorful vegetables, such as carrots, bell peppers, zucchini, and sweet potatoes, with olive oil, salt, and pepper. Roast them in the oven until tender and slightly golden. Roasted vegetables are versatile and can complement a wide range of main courses, adding vibrant colors and nutrients to your plate.

2. Quinoa Pilaf:

Quinoa pilaf is a nutritious and versatile side dish that pairs well with many main courses. Cook quinoa according to package instructions and sauté it with aromatics like onions and garlic. Add in your choice of vegetables, such as peas, diced carrots, or bell peppers, and season with herbs and spices. Quinoa pilaf provides a protein-rich, fiber-packed alternative to traditional rice dishes.

3. Creamy Mashed Cauliflower:

For a lighter and lower-carb alternative to mashed potatoes, try creamy mashed cauliflower. Steam or boil cauliflower florets until tender, then mash them with a touch of butter or olive oil, garlic, and a splash of milk or vegetable broth. Season with salt, pepper, and herbs like chives or parsley. The result is a velvety and flavorful side dish that pairs well with various proteins.

4. Mixed Greens Salad:

A fresh and vibrant mixed greens salad is always a fantastic addition to any meal. Combine a variety of leafy greens, such as spinach, arugula, and romaine lettuce, with colorful vegetables like cherry tomatoes, cucumbers, and bell peppers. Top with your choice of protein, such as grilled chicken or tofu, and finish with a light vinaigrette dressing. A mixed greens salad adds a refreshing and nutrient-rich element to your plate.

5. Herbed Couscous:

Couscous is a quick-cooking and versatile grain that makes an excellent side dish. Prepare couscous according to package instructions and toss it with fresh herbs like parsley, mint, and cilantro. Add diced cucumbers, cherry tomatoes, and lemon zest for a burst of freshness. Couscous pairs well with Mediterranean, Middle Eastern, or North African-inspired main courses.

6. Sautéed Garlic Green Beans:

Sautéed garlic green beans offer a simple yet flavorful side dish. In a skillet, heat olive oil and minced garlic over medium heat until fragrant. Add trimmed green beans and sauté until they are crisp-tender. Season with salt, pepper, and a squeeze of lemon juice. This side dish adds vibrant color, texture, and a burst of garlic flavor to your meal.

7. Baked Sweet Potato Fries:

Swap regular fries with baked sweet potato fries for a healthier alternative. Cut sweet potatoes into thin strips, toss with a little olive oil, and season with your choice of spices, such as paprika, cumin, or garlic powder. Bake in the oven until crispy on the outside and tender on the inside. Baked sweet potato fries offer a delightful combination of sweetness and savory flavors.

Consider the flavors and textures that complement your main course when selecting a side dish. These fantastic side dishes provide a range of options to enhance your meal, adding variety, nutrition, and deliciousness to your plate. Get creative and explore different combinations to find the perfect side dish for your next culinary creation.

CHAPTER THIRTEEN

Decadent Desserts without the Blood Sugar Spike

Indulging in decadent desserts is possible even while managing blood sugar levels. By making thoughtful ingredient choices and using alternative sweeteners, you can enjoy delicious treats without experiencing a significant spike in blood sugar. These desserts not only satisfy your sweet tooth but also incorporate ingredients that promote better blood sugar control. Let's explore some options for decadent desserts that won't cause a blood sugar spike.

1. Fresh Fruit Parfait:

Create a delightful and refreshing dessert by layering fresh fruits with a dollop of Greek yogurt or coconut yogurt. Choose fruits with a lower glycemic index such as berries, cherries, or apples. Top the parfait with a sprinkle of nuts or seeds for added crunch and healthy fats. This dessert provides natural sweetness, fiber, and essential nutrients while keeping blood sugar levels stable.

2. Dark Chocolate Bark:

Dark chocolate with a high cocoa content (70% or higher) contains less sugar and a higher concentration of antioxidants compared to milk chocolate. Melt dark chocolate and spread it on a baking sheet lined with parchment paper. Sprinkle with chopped nuts, dried fruits, or shredded coconut. Allow it to harden in the refrigerator before breaking it into pieces. Dark chocolate bark offers a rich and satisfying treat with moderate sugar content.

3. Chia Pudding:

Chia seeds are a great source of fiber, healthy fats, and protein. Make a chia seed pudding by combining chia seeds with your choice of milk (dairy or plant-based), a natural sweetener like stevia or monk fruit, and flavorings such as vanilla extract or unsweetened cocoa powder. Let it sit in the refrigerator overnight to thicken. Top with fresh berries or a sprinkle of cinnamon for added flavor. Chia pudding is a creamy and nutritious dessert that won't cause a rapid rise in blood sugar.

4. Baked Apples:

Baked apples make for a warm and comforting dessert. Core apples and fill the cavity with a mixture of chopped nuts, cinnamon, and a small amount of natural sweetener like honey or maple syrup. Bake until the apples are tender and the filling is golden and fragrant. Serve with a dollop of Greek yogurt or a drizzle of almond butter for added creaminess and protein.

5. Avocado Chocolate Mousse:

Avocado can be used to create a creamy and rich chocolate mousse without the need for added sugar. Blend ripe avocados with unsweetened cocoa powder, a natural sweetener like stevia or erythritol, a splash of vanilla extract, and a pinch of salt. Adjust the sweetness and consistency to your liking. Refrigerate the mixture until chilled and enjoy a luscious and blood sugar-friendly chocolate mousse.

6. Sugar-Free Cheesecake:

Prepare a sugar-free cheesecake using a combination of cream cheese, Greek yogurt, a sugar substitute like erythritol or stevia, and flavorings such as lemon zest or vanilla extract. Create a crust using crushed nuts or a blend of almond flour and melted butter. Bake until set, then let it cool and chill in the refrigerator before serving. A sugar-free cheesecake allows you to enjoy the creamy and indulgent flavors without the blood sugar spike.

Always remember to enjoy these decadent desserts in moderation and be mindful of portion sizes. Although they are made with alternative sweeteners or lower glycemic index ingredients, they still contribute to overall carbohydrate intake. By making smart ingredient choices and using natural sweeteners, you can satisfy your dessert cravings while maintaining stable blood sugar levels.

CHAPTER FOURTEEN

Savory Sauces, Dressings, and Marinades for Diabetic Cuisine

Sauces, dressings, and marinades are essential elements in adding flavor and enhancing the taste of various dishes. For individuals managing diabetes, it's important to choose options that are low in added sugars, sodium, and unhealthy fats. Luckily, there are plenty of savory alternatives available that can elevate your meals without compromising your blood sugar control. Let's explore some delicious and diabetes-friendly sauces, dressings, and marinades that will bring a burst of flavor to your culinary creations.

1. Balsamic Vinaigrette:

Create a tangy and flavorful dressing using balsamic vinegar, Dijon mustard, garlic, and a touch of olive oil. Whisk the ingredients together until well combined and drizzle over salads or roasted vegetables. Balsamic vinaigrette is a versatile and low-carb option that adds a delightful zing to your dishes.

2. Lemon Herb Sauce:

Make a refreshing and citrusy sauce by combining freshly squeezed lemon juice, minced garlic, chopped fresh herbs (such as parsley, basil, and thyme), and a small amount of olive oil. This sauce pairs well with grilled chicken, fish, or roasted vegetables, infusing them with a burst of vibrant flavors.

3. Greek Yogurt Dip:

Greek yogurt is a fantastic base for creating creamy and flavorful dips. Mix Greek yogurt with herbs like dill, chives, and garlic powder for a tangy and refreshing dip. This versatile dip complements raw vegetables, baked pita chips, or grilled chicken skewers, adding a creamy and protein-rich element to your meal.

4. Tomato Salsa:

Whip up a homemade salsa using fresh tomatoes, onions, jalapeños (if desired), lime juice, and cilantro. This vibrant and zesty salsa can be used as a topping for grilled fish or chicken, as a dip with whole-grain tortilla chips, or as a flavorful addition to wraps and salads. Opt for a homemade version to control the amount of sodium and sugar.

5. Teriyaki Marinade:

Prepare a homemade teriyaki marinade by combining reduced-sodium soy sauce, grated ginger, minced garlic, a touch of honey or a sugar substitute, and a splash of rice vinegar. Use this marinade to flavor lean meats like chicken or salmon before grilling or broiling. The sweet and savory flavors of teriyaki add depth and richness to your dishes.

6. Pesto Sauce:

Create a vibrant pesto sauce by blending fresh basil leaves, garlic, pine nuts, grated Parmesan cheese (or a dairy-free alternative), and a drizzle of olive oil. This versatile sauce can be used as a spread on sandwiches, tossed with whole grain pasta or zucchini noodles, or as a flavorful topping for grilled vegetables. Adjust the amount of oil and cheese to meet your dietary preferences and needs.

7. Tangy Mustard Sauce:

Mix Dijon mustard, apple cider vinegar, a touch of honey or a sugar substitute, and a pinch of salt and pepper to create a tangy and zesty sauce. This versatile sauce can be used as a dipping sauce for grilled meats or as a flavorful topping for salads and roasted vegetables. It adds a tangy kick to your dishes without spiking your blood sugar.

When choosing store-bought options, be sure to read the ingredient labels carefully, looking for low-sodium, low-sugar, and low-fat options. Alternatively, creating your own homemade sauces, dressings, and marinades gives you control over the ingredients and allows for customization to suit your taste preferences.

By incorporating these savory sauces, dressings, and marinades into your diabetic cuisine, you can elevate the flavors of your dishes while keeping your blood sugar levels in check. Remember to practice portion control and balance your meals with wholesome ingredients for optimal diabetes

CHAPTER FIFTEEN

Guilt-Free Snacks and Small Bites for Diabetes Management

When managing diabetes, it's essential to choose snacks and small bites that are satisfying, flavorful, and won't cause a significant spike in blood sugar levels. By opting for guilt-free options that are low in added sugars, refined carbohydrates, and unhealthy fats, you can keep your blood sugar in check while enjoying tasty and nutritious snacks. Let's explore some delicious guilt-free snacks and small bites that are suitable for diabetes management.

1. Veggie Sticks with Hummus:

Crunchy and refreshing, raw vegetable sticks like carrot, celery, and bell pepper are excellent options for a guilt-free snack. Pair them with a serving of homemade or store-bought hummus, which is rich in protein and healthy fats. This combination provides a satisfying and fiber-rich snack that helps stabilize blood sugar levels.

2. Greek Yogurt Parfait:

Indulge in a protein-packed Greek yogurt parfait by layering unsweetened Greek yogurt with fresh berries, a sprinkle of crushed nuts or seeds, and a drizzle of sugar-free or natural sweetener like stevia. This snack offers a balance of protein, fiber, and antioxidants, making it a delicious and filling option.

3. Nuts and Seeds:

Enjoy a handful of nuts and seeds for a satisfying and heart-healthy snack. Almonds, walnuts, pistachios, and pumpkin seeds are great choices. These nutrient-dense snacks provide a good source of healthy fats, protein, and fiber. Remember to stick to a small portion size to control calorie intake.

4. Hard-Boiled Eggs:

Hard-boiled eggs are an easy and portable snack that offers protein, healthy fats, and essential vitamins and minerals. Keep a few hard-boiled eggs in the refrigerator for a quick and satiating snack option.

5. Cheese and Whole Grain Crackers:

Pair a small portion of low-fat cheese with whole grain crackers for a satisfying snack that combines protein, calcium, and fiber. Look for crackers with minimal added sugars and made from whole grains like whole wheat or rye.

6. Sliced Apple with Peanut Butter:

Slice up a crisp apple and enjoy it with a dollop of natural peanut butter. Apples provide fiber and antioxidants, while peanut butter offers protein and healthy fats. This combination is both delicious and nutritious.

7. Homemade Trail Mix:

Create your own customized trail mix using a mix of unsalted nuts, seeds, and a small portion of dried fruits like cranberries or apricots. Be mindful of portion sizes, as dried fruits can be higher in natural sugars.

8. Roasted Chickpeas:

Roasted chickpeas make a crunchy and protein-rich snack. Toss rinsed and drained chickpeas with olive oil, salt, and your preferred seasonings like paprika, garlic powder, or cumin. Roast in the oven until golden and crispy. They can be enjoyed on their own or added to salads for an extra crunch.

9. Cucumber and Tuna Bites:

Slice cucumber into rounds and top each slice with a small spoonful of canned tuna mixed with Greek yogurt, lemon juice, and herbs. These bite-sized snacks are refreshing, low in carbohydrates, and provide a good amount of protein.

10. Homemade Vegetable Chips:

Create your own baked vegetable chips using thinly sliced vegetables like zucchini, kale, or beetroot. Toss the slices with a small amount of olive oil, season with herbs or spices, and bake until crispy. These homemade chips offer a satisfying crunch while being lower in calories and carbohydrates compared to traditional potato chips.

Monitor portion sizes and pay attention to the overall balance of your meals and snacks. These guilt-free snacks and small bites provide a variety of flavors and textures while helping you maintain stable blood sugar levels. Enjoy them as part of a well-rounded and balanced diet, and consult with a healthcare professional or registered dietitian for personalized guidance in managing your diabetes.

CHAPTER SIXTEEN

Celebratory Menus: Special Occasion Recipes for Diabetics

Special occasions and celebrations are meant to be enjoyed, and having diabetes shouldn't stop you from savoring delicious meals on these memorable days. With a bit of planning and creativity, you can create celebratory menus that are both festive and diabetes-friendly. Here are some ideas for special occasion recipes that will satisfy your taste buds while keeping your blood sugar levels in check.

Appetizers:

1. **Caprese Skewers:**
   Skewer fresh cherry tomatoes, mozzarella balls, and basil leaves. Drizzle with balsamic reduction for a flavorful and visually appealing appetizer.

2. **Smoked Salmon Roll-Ups:**
Spread a thin layer of cream cheese on smoked salmon slices, then roll them up with cucumber or avocado. Slice into bite-sized pieces for an elegant and protein-packed appetizer.

Main Courses:

1. **Grilled Herb-Crusted Salmon:**
Season salmon fillets with a mixture of fresh herbs, garlic, and lemon zest. Grill or bake until cooked through and serve with a side of roasted vegetables or a refreshing salad.
2. **Lemon Herb Roasted Chicken:**
Roast a whole chicken with a blend of lemon, garlic, rosemary, and thyme. The result is a tender and flavorful centerpiece for your celebratory meal.
3. **Beef Tenderloin with Mushroom Sauce:**
Grill or roast beef tenderloin to perfection and serve with a savory

mushroom sauce made from low-sodium beef broth, mushrooms, and a splash of red wine. Pair it with steamed asparagus or a medley of roasted vegetables.

Side Dishes:

1. **Roasted Brussels Sprouts with Balsamic Glaze:**
Roast Brussels sprouts with a drizzle of olive oil, salt, and pepper until caramelized. Finish them off with a balsamic glaze for a tangy and irresistible side dish.
2. **Quinoa Pilaf:**
Cook quinoa with low-sodium vegetable broth and toss it with sautéed vegetables like bell peppers, zucchini, and onions. Add herbs like parsley or cilantro for an extra burst of freshness.
3. **Cauliflower Mash:**
Steam or boil cauliflower until tender, then blend until smooth. Season with

garlic powder, a touch of low-fat Greek yogurt, and sprinkle with chopped chives. This creamy and low-carb alternative to mashed potatoes pairs well with many main dishes.

Desserts:

1. **Berry Parfait:**
   Layer fresh berries with sugar-free whipped cream or low-fat Greek yogurt. Top with a sprinkle of crushed nuts or a drizzle of sugar-free chocolate sauce for an elegant and guilt-free dessert.
2. **Flourless Chocolate Cake:**
   Bake a rich and decadent flourless chocolate cake using a sugar substitute like stevia or erythritol. Serve it with a dollop of unsweetened whipped cream or a side of fresh berries.

3. **Grilled Pineapple with Cinnamon:**
   Grill pineapple slices until they caramelize and become slightly charred. Sprinkle with cinnamon and serve with a scoop of sugar-free vanilla ice cream or a dollop of Greek yogurt for a tropical and satisfying dessert.

Don't forget to pay attention to portion sizes, as even diabetes-friendly dishes can contribute to blood sugar fluctuations when consumed in excess. Additionally, individual dietary needs and preferences may vary, so it's always a good idea to consult with a healthcare professional or registered dietitian for personalized advice and guidance.

By incorporating these special occasion recipes into your celebratory menus, you can enjoy memorable meals while managing your diabetes and ensuring that the occasion remains both festive and health-conscious.

CHAPTER SEVENTEEN

Kid-Friendly Fare: Nurturing Diabetic Diets for Children

Nurturing a diabetic diet for children can be a rewarding and essential part of helping them manage their condition and maintain optimal health. While it may require some adjustments and creativity, providing kid-friendly fare that is balanced, nutritious, and diabetes-friendly can ensure that children enjoy delicious meals while keeping their blood sugar levels stable. Here are some tips and ideas for nurturing diabetic diets for children:

1. Emphasize Whole Foods:

Focus on incorporating whole foods into your child's meals. Include plenty of fresh fruits, vegetables, lean proteins, whole grains, and healthy fats. These nutrient-dense foods provide essential vitamins, minerals, and fiber while helping to stabilize blood sugar levels.

2. Opt for Complex Carbohydrates:

Choose complex carbohydrates instead of simple carbohydrates. Whole grains like whole wheat bread, brown rice, quinoa, and oatmeal have a lower impact on blood sugar levels compared to refined grains. These carbohydrates are also higher in fiber, which aids in digestion and helps to regulate blood sugar.

3. Incorporate Protein:

Including protein in each meal helps to slow down the absorption of carbohydrates, preventing rapid spikes in blood sugar levels. Lean sources of protein such as skinless poultry, fish, beans, tofu, and Greek yogurt are excellent choices. Consider making protein a central component of meals, as it provides sustained energy and promotes satiety.

4. Offer Balanced Snacks:

Provide balanced snacks that combine carbohydrates, protein, and healthy fats. For example, pair apple slices with a small amount of peanut butter or offer whole-grain crackers with low-fat cheese. These snacks provide sustained energy and prevent blood sugar fluctuations between meals.

5. Make It Fun and Engaging:

Engage children in the meal planning and preparation process. Let them choose fruits and vegetables they enjoy and involve them in simple tasks such as washing produce or stirring ingredients. Present meals in a visually appealing manner, using colorful plates and fun-shaped food items to make the experience enjoyable and exciting.

6. Limit Added Sugars:

Minimize the consumption of added sugars in your child's diet. Be mindful of hidden sugars in processed foods and opt for natural sources of sweetness such as fresh fruits. Avoid sugary drinks and offer water, unsweetened milk, or homemade smoothies as healthier alternatives.

7. Control Portion Sizes:

Monitor portion sizes to avoid overeating. Use smaller plates and bowls to create the illusion of a fuller plate. Encourage children to eat slowly, savor their food, and listen to their body's cues of hunger and fullness.

8. Educate and Communicate:

Teach children about diabetes and the importance of making healthy food choices. Explain the impact of different foods on their blood sugar levels and empower them to make informed decisions. Foster open communication and create a supportive environment where they feel comfortable discussing their dietary needs and concerns.

9. Be a Role Model:

Lead by example and demonstrate healthy eating habits yourself. When children see their caregivers making nutritious choices, they are more likely to follow suit. Encourage family meals and make them an opportunity for bonding and sharing experiences.

10. Seek Professional Guidance:

Consult with a healthcare professional or a registered dietitian who specializes in pediatric diabetes for personalized guidance and meal planning. They can provide tailored recommendations and address specific concerns related to your child's individual needs.

By nurturing diabetic diets for children with a focus on whole foods, balanced meals, and engaging experiences, you can help them develop healthy eating habits and manage their condition effectively. Remember, every child is unique, so it's important to work together with healthcare professionals to create a plan that suits your child's specific needs and preferences.

CHAPTER EIGHTEEN

Seasonal Delights: Recipes Inspired by Fresh Produce

Seasonal delights inspired by fresh produce are not only a delicious way to explore the flavors of each season but also a fantastic way to nourish your body with nutrient-rich ingredients. When you align your recipes with the seasons, you can enjoy the freshest fruits, vegetables, and herbs, which are often at their peak in terms of flavor and nutritional value. Let's dive into the concept of seasonal cooking and explore some recipe ideas that will truly delight your taste buds.

1. Spring:

Spring brings a bounty of fresh greens, tender vegetables, and fragrant herbs. Embrace the vibrant flavors of the season with recipes like:
- Asparagus and Spinach Salad with Lemon Vinaigrette

- Pea and Mint Soup
- Strawberry and Spinach Salad with Balsamic Glaze
- Roasted Spring Vegetables with Herbs

2. Summer:

Summer is synonymous with an abundance of colorful fruits and vegetables. Take advantage of the summer produce with recipes such as:
- Caprese Salad with Heirloom Tomatoes and Fresh Basil
- Grilled Corn and Black Bean Salad
- Watermelon and Feta Salad with Mint
- Grilled Vegetable Skewers with a Balsamic Glaze

3. Fall:

As the weather cools down, fall brings a harvest of hearty vegetables, apples, and warming spices. Embrace the cozy flavors of fall with recipes like:

- Butternut Squash Soup with Cinnamon and Nutmeg
- Roasted Brussels Sprouts with Cranberries and Pecans
- Apple and Kale Salad with Maple Dijon Dressing
- Pumpkin and Chickpea Curry

4. Winter:

Winter calls for comforting dishes that make use of root vegetables, citrus fruits, and robust herbs and spices. Enjoy the cozy flavors of winter with recipes such as:
- Roasted Root Vegetable Medley with Rosemary
- Citrus and Avocado Salad
- Roasted Cauliflower Soup with Turmeric and Ginger
- Spiced Baked Apples with Cinnamon and Nutmeg

Remember to adapt these recipes to suit your dietary needs and preferences, including any modifications required for managing diabetes. Here are a few general tips for incorporating fresh produce into your seasonal cooking:

a. Visit local farmers' markets or join a community-supported agriculture (CSA) program to access the freshest seasonal produce.
b. Experiment with new fruits and vegetables that you may not have tried before. This expands your culinary repertoire and adds variety to your meals.
c. Preserve seasonal produce for later use by freezing, canning, or making homemade jams and sauces.
d. Incorporate fresh herbs into your recipes to enhance flavors without adding excess salt or unhealthy seasonings.
e. Be creative with your cooking methods. Try grilling, roasting, sautéing, or even enjoying certain fruits and vegetables raw to highlight their natural flavors.

By embracing seasonal delights and recipes inspired by fresh produce, you can savor the best flavors each season has to offer. This approach not only enhances your culinary experience but also ensures that you're nourishing your body with the freshest and most nutritious ingredients available. Enjoy the journey of exploring seasonal cooking and the wonderful flavors it brings to your table.

CHAPTER NINETEEN

Quick and Easy Meals for Busy Diabetics

For busy individuals managing diabetes, finding quick and easy meal options that are nutritious and blood sugar-friendly is essential. With a little planning and some simple strategies, you can prepare meals that are both convenient and supportive of your diabetes management. Here are some ideas for quick and easy meals that will keep you satisfied and on track:

1. Stir-Fry Delight:

Stir-fries are versatile, quick to prepare, and allow you to incorporate a variety of vegetables. Choose lean proteins like chicken, shrimp, or tofu and sauté them with an assortment of colorful veggies such as bell peppers, broccoli, and snap peas. Season with low-sodium soy sauce or a flavorful stir-fry sauce. Serve over a small portion of brown rice or quinoa for a balanced meal.

2. Salad in a Jar:

Prepare salad ingredients in advance and store them in mason jars for easy grab-and-go lunches or dinners. Start with a base of leafy greens like spinach or mixed greens, then layer on protein sources such as grilled chicken, chickpeas, or hard-boiled eggs. Add a variety of chopped vegetables, nuts or seeds, and a dressing of your choice. When ready to eat, simply shake the jar to mix the ingredients together.

3. One-Pan Roasted Meals:

Streamline your cooking process by preparing complete meals on a single sheet pan. Toss your choice of protein (chicken breasts, fish fillets, or tofu cubes) with a variety of vegetables like Brussels sprouts, cherry tomatoes, and zucchini. Drizzle with olive oil, sprinkle with herbs and spices, and roast in the oven until everything is cooked through. This approach minimizes clean-up while providing a balanced and flavorful meal.

4. Wraps and Roll-Ups:

Choose whole-grain tortillas or lettuce leaves as a base for creating delicious wraps and roll-ups. Fill them with lean proteins like turkey, chicken, or grilled vegetables, and add a variety of fresh veggies and a smear of hummus or avocado for extra flavor. These portable and customizable meals are perfect for busy days.

5. Quick Soups:

Prepare simple and nourishing soups in a short amount of time. Choose low-sodium broth as a base and add lean proteins such as diced chicken or tofu, along with a mix of vegetables and herbs. Simmer until the flavors meld together, and you have a comforting and satisfying meal.

6. Overnight Oats:

Prepare a batch of overnight oats the night before to enjoy a hassle-free breakfast. Combine rolled oats with your choice of milk (dairy or plant-based), add a touch of sweetness with a sugar substitute like stevia or a drizzle of honey, and mix in toppings such as fresh berries, chopped nuts, or a sprinkle of cinnamon. Let it sit in the refrigerator overnight, and it will be ready to eat in the morning.

7. Egg Muffins:

Whisk together eggs, your favorite vegetables (spinach, bell peppers, mushrooms), and a small amount of low-fat cheese. Pour the mixture into muffin tins and bake until set. These mini frittatas can be made in advance and stored in the refrigerator for a quick grab-and-go breakfast or snack.

8. Quick and Easy Salads:

Combine pre-washed salad greens with a protein source such as grilled chicken, canned tuna, or beans. Add sliced cucumbers, cherry tomatoes, and any other desired vegetables. Top with a sprinkle of seeds or nuts for added crunch and a drizzle of homemade vinaigrette made with olive oil, vinegar, and herbs.

9. Smoothie Bowls:

Blend together a combination of frozen fruits, a handful of leafy greens, a source of protein like Greek yogurt or a scoop of protein powder, and a liquid such as almond milk or water. Pour the smoothie into a bowl and top it with nutritious add-ons like chia seeds, sliced fruit, or granola for a satisfying and quick meal.

10. Healthy Freezer Meals:

Prepare larger batches of healthy meals when you have some extra time, and store individual portions in the freezer. This way, you'll always have a quick and nutritious meal on hand when you're short on time. Soups, stews, casseroles, and chili are great options for freezer-friendly meals.

While these meals are quick and convenient, it's important to prioritize nutrition and portion control. Be mindful of your carbohydrate intake and choose whole, unprocessed ingredients whenever possible. Consulting with a healthcare professional or registered dietitian can help you personalize your meal plan and ensure it aligns with your specific dietary needs and diabetes management goals.

By incorporating these quick and easy meal ideas into your routine, you can maintain a healthy and balanced diet while managing a busy schedule.

CHAPTER TWENTY

Dining Out the Diabetic Way: Tips and Tricks for Restaurant Success

Dining out can be an enjoyable experience, even when you're managing diabetes. With some knowledge and planning, you can navigate restaurant menus and make choices that support your blood sugar management goals. Here are some tips and tricks for dining out the diabetic way:

1. Plan Ahead:

If possible, review the restaurant's menu online before your visit. Look for options that are lower in carbohydrates, such as grilled or roasted proteins, steamed vegetables, and salads. Knowing what to expect will help you make informed choices when you arrive.

2. Watch Portion Sizes:

Restaurant portions tend to be larger than what you might typically consume at home. Consider sharing a dish with a dining companion or ask for a to-go container at the beginning of the meal and pack away half of your entrée for later. This helps you control your portion sizes and manage your carbohydrate intake.

3. Be Mindful of Hidden Sugars:

Many restaurant dishes contain added sugars that can affect your blood sugar levels. Avoid dishes with sweet sauces, glazes, or dressings. Instead, opt for simple preparations or ask for sauces and dressings on the side, allowing you to control the amount you consume.

4. Choose High-Fiber Options:

Fiber-rich foods can help slow down the absorption of glucose and promote better blood sugar control. Look for menu items that include whole grains, legumes, and non-starchy vegetables. These options provide important nutrients and help you feel fuller for longer.

5. Opt for Grilled, Baked, or Steamed:

When it comes to preparation methods, choose grilled, baked, or steamed dishes over fried or breaded options. These methods minimize added fats and reduce the overall calorie content of your meal while still delivering great flavor.

6. Request Modifications:

Don't be afraid to ask for modifications to suit your dietary needs. Most restaurants are accommodating and willing to make adjustments. For example, request a side of vegetables instead of starchy sides like fries or mashed potatoes. Ask for sauces and dressings to be served on the side or omitted altogether.

7. Control Your Beverages:

Be mindful of your beverage choices, as many sugary drinks can cause blood sugar spikes. Opt for water, unsweetened iced tea, or sparkling water with a twist of lemon or lime. If you choose to have an alcoholic beverage, do so in moderation and select lower-sugar options like light beer or dry wine.

8. Enjoy Mindfully:

Practice mindful eating by savoring each bite, chewing slowly, and paying attention to your body's hunger and fullness cues. This can help prevent overeating and allow you to enjoy your meal more fully.

9. Don't Skip Meals:

If you know you'll be dining out later in the day, don't skip meals earlier in the day. This can lead to excessive hunger and overeating later on. Instead, have balanced meals and snacks throughout the day to keep your blood sugar stable.

10. Be Prepared:

Consider keeping some diabetes-friendly snacks in your bag or car in case the restaurant options don't align with your dietary needs. This way, you can manage your blood sugar while enjoying the social aspect of dining out.

It's important to work closely with your healthcare team, including a registered dietitian, to develop a personalized eating plan that suits your specific needs. They can provide guidance on carbohydrate counting, portion control, and other strategies to help you navigate dining out successfully.

By employing these tips and tricks, you can enjoy dining out while maintaining control over your blood sugar levels and supporting your overall diabetes management goals.

CONCLUSION

Throughout this book, we have explored a wide array of delicious, nutritious, and diabetes-friendly recipes that prove that managing blood sugar doesn't mean sacrificing flavor or culinary creativity.

By combining the art of gourmet cooking with the science of blood sugar control, we have shown that it is possible to enjoy gourmet meals while maintaining stable glucose levels. From the tantalizing appetizers to the mouthwatering main courses and delectable desserts, each recipe has been meticulously crafted to provide a harmonious balance of taste, nutrition, and blood sugar management.

We have delved into various aspects of diabetic nutrition, including the importance of understanding carbohydrates, portion control, and mindful eating. By offering detailed nutritional information and practical tips, we have empowered you to make informed choices and take control of your dietary habits. With the knowledge gained from this book, you can confidently navigate the culinary landscape, adapting recipes to suit your preferences and nutritional needs.

Furthermore, we have emphasized the significance of fresh, whole ingredients and mindful cooking techniques. By focusing on quality ingredients and employing cooking methods that preserve both taste and nutrients, we have showcased the power of wholesome cooking in promoting overall health and wellbeing.

This book is more than just a collection of recipes. It is a guidebook that equips you with the tools, knowledge, and inspiration to embrace a gourmet approach to diabetic cooking. It is a celebration of the joy and satisfaction that can be found in creating delicious meals that not only nourish the body but also delight the senses.

As you embark on your culinary adventures, remember that each meal is an opportunity to savor the flavors, nurture your body, and make positive choices that support your journey towards optimal health. Whether you are a seasoned chef or a novice in the kitchen, this book serves as your companion, offering a treasure trove of gourmet dishes and culinary wisdom to enhance your diabetic lifestyle.

May this book inspire you to embark on a lifelong journey of culinary creativity, where every meal becomes an exquisite masterpiece designed to nourish your body, please your palate, and empower you to live a vibrant life with diabetes. Remember, with passion, knowledge, and the right ingredients, you can transform your kitchen into a sanctuary of culinary delight and embrace a delicious, balanced, and diabetes-friendly way of life.

Made in United States
North Haven, CT
14 June 2024